Proceeds from the sale of this book go to our
Franciscan Mission in Zimbabwe.

Please send correspondence to:
The Simplest Prayer
Franciscan Friars, 4 Merchants' Quay, Dublin 8, Ireland
OR
simplestprayer@franciscans.ie

THE SIMPLEST PRAYER

A BOOK OF LOVE AND FAITH

THE IRISH FRANCISCANS

HACHETTE
BOOKS
IRELAND

First published in 2014 by Hachette Books Ireland

2

Copyright © The Irish Franciscans 2014

A CIP catalogue record for this title is available from the British Library.

ISBN: 9781444799996

Book Design and Typesetting by Anú Design
Printed and bound by Clays Ltd, St Ives plc

Hachette Books Ireland policy is to use papers that are natural, renewable
and recyclable products and made from wood grown in sustainable forests.
The logging and manufacturing processes are expected to conform to the
environmental regulations of the country of origin.

Hachette Books Ireland
8 Castlecourt Centre, Castleknock, Dublin 15, Ireland

A division of Hachette UK Ltd
338 Euston Road, London NW1 3BH
www.hachette.ie

Contents

❖

❖

Who is Jesus?

❖

Reaching Out to Jesus

✤

The How of Praying: Some Suggestions

✤

Prayers to Encircle Each Day

Whatever you do, whether in word or deed, do it all in the Name of the Lord Jesus, giving thanks to God the Father through him. ✍

Colossians 3:17

Invoking Jesus!

Jesus, yours is the name above all names:
We offer you our heartfelt praise and gratitude.
Deepen in us an abiding reverence
For your Holy Name.

Jesus, Saviour, heal the wounds within
That our sin and fear have inflicted.
Set us free from all that hinders us,
Rejoicing in your boundless love
And sharing your goodness with others.

Jesus, Friend, draw us ever closer to you.
We entrust all we carry in our hearts
To your abundant mercy.

Jesus, Lord, pour out the Holy Spirit
Upon your people
That our lives may overflow with your grace,
Our days be filled with your love,
And all our actions shine with your light.

Amen

(Composed for the Year of the Holy Name)

Foreword

✥

Francis of Assisi was a man whose heart was enthralled and whose mind was captivated by the person of Jesus. His first biographer, Friar Thomas of Celano, wrote: 'He was always with Jesus: Jesus in his heart, Jesus in his mouth, Jesus in his ears, Jesus in his eyes, Jesus in his hands; he bore Jesus always in his whole body.'

Francis rejoiced that the Lord was 'the fullness of good, all good, every good, the true and supreme good'.

In keeping with our Franciscan tradition, these pages, written by an Irish friar, attempt to present with clarity the beauty and the goodness of the Lord, that we might be drawn to him by attraction.

The simplest prayer is to reach out in faith to him whose love and mercy will never fail us.

It is appropriate that this book appears during the Year of the Holy Name of Jesus when the Franciscan family in Ireland celebrates the centenary of the revival of devotion to the Holy Name begun in 1914. In a certain sense, it is a follow-on publication to *Calm the Soul*, the very popular book from our sisters, the Poor Clares in Galway.

May all who read this book be drawn closer to the Lord Jesus in heartfelt trust; may they experience anew the grace of his presence and know with joy the gift of his love in their lives.

Hugh McKenna, OFM
Provincial Minister
Franciscan Province of Ireland

Introduction:
The Simplest Prayer

✤

The Lord is near to all who call upon him.
Psalms 145:18

There is nothing we can do to make God love us more. There is nothing we can do to make God love us less. We are loved – simply, completely and eternally. In Jesus, this love has come so close to us. He became one of us, our brother. He loved and laughed, suffered and struggled. And in him is found all the fullness and goodness of divine love.

The simplest prayer is to call out to Jesus in our need, to invoke his name with trust in any time or place – no matter how weak we feel our faith is, no matter what our present circumstances or our past deeds. 'Everyone who calls upon the name of the Lord will be saved' (Romans 10:13). Pronouncing the Holy Name of Jesus with love and trust is the shortest of prayers, the simplest prayer. In a busy world such as our own, we can find ourselves in difficult situations unexpectedly. The name of Jesus, spoken with love and reverence, can be a source of comfort and support in these situations when all else fails.

Jesus is our friend and helper on life's journey. He cares about our every need and loves us unfailingly and constantly. Calling on his name makes him present to us in a very real way. He wants to effect in our lives what his name means; he wants to save us. It is a particular blessing to have the name of Jesus on our lips as we pass from this world to the next.

If we are struggling, he is here for us and all who are bruised and battered by life. If we are painfully aware of the mess in our circumstances or family, he is here for us, when we know of our desperate need of God. And if we are weighted down by our mistakes and failures, he is here to lift us up, as often as we need to be lifted up.

He knows us through and through and loves us as deeply as he knows us. Our brokenness stirs his heart. 'The Lord upholds all those who fall and lifts up all who are bowed down' (Psalms 145:14). Then, secure in his goodness, we ourselves are enabled to love others generously.

This book is for those burdened by questions arising from our lives: Where do I find strength and guidance for daily living? How can I connect with God? What do I really believe? How can I deepen the faith I have? Who or what can free me from the obsessions and fears that at times can control my thoughts and my days? The Lord is near to all who call upon him. May these reflections help us to experience the radical depth of his tender love for us. And may we know a blossoming of hope and joy before the sublime gift that is Jesus.

The living words of Jesus have a divine energy to touch our hearts. They can stir up our trust in him, unshackle the soul and unwrap the heart to grace. The reflections in this book are based on the Gospels. When pondered prayerfully, they enable Jesus to speak to us directly.

The question is not: Does the Lord love me? The issue is our openness to his love. So the crucial question is: How deeply, how freely, how powerfully do I allow that divine love to enter in and transform my life? The more I lower my defences – the more I let his love in – then the more I experience his power at work in my life. Love cannot force itself. The Lord will wait humbly for my consent.

This book was written during the Year of the Holy Name, as the Franciscan family in Ireland celebrates the centenary of the renewal of devotion to the name of Jesus, begun in the country in 1914. At the heart of the year is the belief that there is power and grace in the very name of Jesus. 'There is no other name under heaven given to men by which we must be saved' (Acts 4:12). The core of the simplest prayer is reaching out in faith to 'touch' Jesus as we call on his name; to draw strength, light and healing from him whatever our situation. 'The Lord is close to the broken-hearted and saves those who are crushed in spirit' (Psalms 34:18). Not everything will be solved or sorted, but we can be so graced with fresh hope and courage and love that life does not overwhelm us or embitter us.

This book has one hope – that it will help us open ourselves to Jesus and his abundant love so that, little by little, it permeates our lives and sets us free.

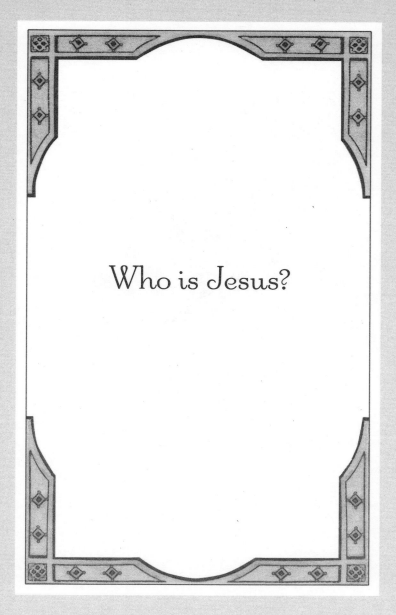

Who is Jesus?

Introduction

✤

We believe that the 'simplest' prayer is to call upon the name of Jesus, to reach out in simple trust to draw life from him. Even simply saying his name consciously calls him into our lives and the moment we are in.

But who is this Jesus we are reaching out to? Who is Jesus for me? To whom am I praying? The more we know him, the more we are able to trust him and reach out to him.

Our understanding of the Lord is crucial to how we relate to him. If we see him as indifferent and aloof, we will not be drawn to him. We do not want to spend time with someone we are afraid of. Nor will we be drawn to someone we resent. There is no joy in coming before someone in whose presence we sense ourselves condemned.

Is Jesus primarily a judge or a saviour for me? Is the Lord to whom I pray faithful in love, constant and reliable, or is he temperamental and moody? Is he patient and compassionate, or hard and judgemental? Is Jesus interested in my world or is he indifferent to the stuff of my daily living?

Our answers to these fundamental questions will decide how close we want to get to the Lord, how at ease we are with him, whether we can look him in the eye or not, whether we can surrender in peaceful trust to his dreams for us or hold on for dear life so that he does not have his way in our lives.

We have different titles for Jesus – Emmanuel, Saviour, Lord and many more. These titles express who he is, and who he wants to be for us. Fully human, he understands us and has compassion on our weaknesses and knows the burdens we carry. The following are some simple reflections, based on the Gospels, which might help us identify and experience all that Jesus wants to be for us, and all that he can be in our lives: friend, brother, confidant, healer.

No one was ever warmed studying the definition of fire; no one ever got drunk reading about red wine. Words are not enough. The Lord invites us to go beyond theory to experience! He wants us to be warmed by the radiant fire of his love, and to drink deeply of the rich wine of his Spirit.

God With Us

✤

When an angel of the Lord appeared to Joseph, Joseph learned that the child to be born to Mary had his origins in the vast mystery of God. He was told:

Joseph, son of David, do not be afraid to take Mary home as your wife, because what is conceived in her is from the Holy Spirit . . . All this took place to fulfil what the Lord had said through the prophet. The virgin will conceive and give birth to a son, and they will call him Emmanuel (which means 'God with us').

Matthew 1:20–23

Indeed, Mary did give birth to a son and he was called Emmanuel – God with us, God among us, God for us. Just as we were born to a mother and a father, so too was Jesus, and this was God's greatest gift to us. He was given as our companion and support on life's path.

In God's complete gift of himself to us in Jesus, we can glimpse his infinite love. We can also see how great our hope and desire can and should be as we come in prayer before Emmanuel.

We can pray for many things – for health, financial issues, our various concerns. There is nothing wrong with this. In fact, the problem lies in our desiring too little. At times, our prayers and our hope are too paltry; our God is too small! To put it simply – God became human so that we humans could become divine. Our entire Christian life is one long birthing into divine life, a life that already dwells within us by the gift of the Holy Spirit. We are asked to experience what is already given, to become what we already are.

Jesus being born to Mary is one of the greatest miracles and, in this act, we learn that anything is possible for God. Jesus wants us to expand our desire. In faith, we must make God's generosity, not our littleness, the measure of our expectations.

Jesus desires to fill us with his own life and love and joy. We are called to light our lives from the flame of his divine life. He asks us not to settle for too little, too soon, when so much is offered to us.

✤✤✤✤✤

GOD WITH US

Jesus, Emmanuel,
help me make space in my life
for the gift of God. ✒

Our brother

✥

We do not often think of Jesus as our brother. But he was and is fully human. Jesus descended into the depths of our human condition. He knows our trials and sorrows; he felt our tiredness and tasted our tears. In Gethsemane, he experienced real fear and distress at the death he was to die for us. 'Jesus said to his disciples, "Sit here while I pray." He took Peter, James and John along with him, and he began to be deeply distressed and troubled. "My soul is overwhelmed with sorrow to the point of death," he said to them. "Stay here and keep watch"' (Mark 14:32–34). He needed his friends' support in his terrible struggle. This was not play-acting.

Jesus, our brother, understands us, our troubles and sufferings. This gives us confidence in coming to him.

For we do not have a high priest who is unable to empathise with our weaknesses, but we have one who has been tempted in every way, just as we are — yet he did not sin. Let us then approach God's throne of grace with confidence, so that we may receive mercy and find grace to help us in our time of need.

Hebrews 4:15–16

However, some of us can be burdened with perfectionism. Then we try to deny our weaknesses or become discouraged when we experience our needs and flaws. At these times, our inner voice can become the voice of the oppressor, stirring up shame and self-contempt because we have failed to live up to certain standards.

The sweetest grace is to allow Jesus' love to make us loveable in our own eyes, to consent to his radical acceptance for us so it becomes the bedrock of our own self-acceptance, and to let his very humanity ignite in our hearts compassion for ourselves and for all others.

✣✣✣✣✣

OUR BROTHER

Jesus, my brother,
in the embrace of your
compassionate knowing
may I befriend my full self. ✎

Our saviour

❖

With Jesus the Saviour, there is always the possibility of fresh starts in our lives. With Christ, every moment can be a new beginning. Jesus can see how we suffer if we are not living to our true potential, even if we do not realise it. He longs to lift us up from the tangle of fear and distress, from the mire of resentment and anger and from the dust of sin and wrong. He delights in being our Saviour.

I have loved you with an everlasting love; I have drawn you with loving-kindness. I will build you up again and you will be rebuilt.
Jeremiah 31:3–4

Jesus is the saving, liberating love of God made real among us, coming in person to set us free.

On the night of his birth, the angels told the shepherds: 'Do not be afraid. I bring you good news that will cause great joy for all the people. Today in the town of David, a Saviour has been born to you; he is the Messiah, the Lord'

Luke 2:10–11

The shepherds were the first to hear the joyful news of the Saviour's birth. The very name Jesus means 'God saves'. It was the name given before his birth 'because he will save his people from their sins' (Matthew 1:21).

✤✤✤✤

OUR SAVIOUR

Jesus, help me give you
the freedom to be a Saviour
to me – a liberating presence
in my life. ∂

Our healer

✤

The Gospels are full of accounts of Jesus healing people. These healings are the tangible sign of the breaking in of God's powerful goodness, restoring our world.

And wherever he went – into villages, towns or countryside – they placed the sick in the marketplaces. They begged him to let them touch even the edge of his cloak, and all who touched it were healed.

Mark 6:56

We are told the glory of God is the human person fully alive. Christ wants to heal us from all that stops us being truly alive in our humanity. He wants us open to God and others in truth and love in the light of his grace. His love reaches even where our own love does not go. God's children are made for life – the fullness of life.

Jesus knows that our inner wounds, such as self-doubt, insecurity and regret, and the hurts we carry can stunt our lives much more than our physical ailments.

There is no sin so great, no hurt so deep, no sorrow so terrible and no fear so gripping that they can be outside the love and grace and healing energy that flow from the Lord.

To touch Jesus is to touch divine compassion and to be renewed in our very humanity.

❖❖❖❖❖

OUR HEALER

Jesus, in faith I reach out
to touch you; help me to
open my whole self –
body, mind and soul –
to your healing power. ℘

Our constant friend

✤

Those who were despised as sinners flocked to Jesus. He was the friend of sinners and they knew it. In his loving companionship, they knew themselves to be more loved than they had dared hope.

Those who deserve love least need love most! To be loved in our virtue is wonderful, but to be loved in our failure and sin is a liberating, joyous experience.

Whoever comes to me I will never drive away.
John 6:37

Jesus knows you cannot build on shame and blame. Nothing new happens without forgiveness. We flourish in an atmosphere of gentleness and compassion. Our hearts wither and our souls dry up in an atmosphere of condemnation and harshness.

The Lord's love for us does not necessarily mean approval for everything in our lives. But that same love gives us both the desire and the power to change.

The miracle of divine love is the capacity never to despair of anyone, to keep on forgiving and to know how to wait with humble love. Jesus stands with those who struggle and fail and fall. He cares for us with an inexhaustible patience. So we should never give up on ourselves, never give up on others, because Jesus never gives up on us.

Many tax collectors and 'sinners' were among Jesus' disciples, and when asked why he was friends with them and eating with them, Jesus replied, 'It is not the healthy who need a doctor, but those who are ill. I have not come to call the righteous, but sinners' (Mark 2:17).

✤✤✤✤✤

Our constant friend

Jesus, help me to know you
as the friend of sinners,
the seeker of the lost,
the giver of new beginnings. ⌒

Our shepherd
and guide

❖

We can wander off and get lost in the darkness, trapped in situations that degrade us, repeating destructive behaviours that rob us of joy. And Jesus comes searching for us.

He has patient compassion when we search for love and happiness in the wrong places. He sees the silent despair, often cloaked in the rush and glitter of life. Our very need draws his goodness. There is no trace of resentment in his great heart at our messy, confused lives. His compassion is unfailing.

Jesus knows us as we are and loves us as we are – even as he draws us deeper into freedom and generosity. The Good Shepherd tells us: 'I have come that they may have life, and have it to the full' (John 10:10). Jesus told the parable of the shepherd who left ninety-nine of his sheep to search for the lost one: 'And when he finds it, he joyfully puts it on his shoulders and goes home' (Luke 15:5).

Those listening to Jesus would have thought, *what a stupid shepherd!* All that fuss about one lost sheep. Leaving ninety-nine sheep to search for one simply made no sense. But that one, and each one, means the world to this Shepherd God.

Jesus wants us to understand how far his love compels him to come in search of us. And at what a cost to himself does he carry us home. God's love for us has made him do foolish things! If we are seeking the Lord, much more is Jesus seeking his beloved. And he intends to pursue his seeking to the very limit.

✤✤✤✤✤

OUR SHEPHERD AND GUIDE

Jesus, shepherd
my days and lead me
to the fullness of life.

Our sustaining bread of life

✤

Jesus is our nourishment. He has become the Bread broken for the life of the world. He wants us to draw life from him. In the very manner of the Lord's coming to us, we see the extent of his love for us. Nothing is held back. 'This is my Body given up for you' (Luke 22:19).

This ultimate gift sums up his entire life and mission – Jesus surrenders all for us and to us. In the Eucharist, we celebrate a love that is poured out freely and without measure. We are sharers in a goodness no indifference can lessen, no sin can quench and no betrayal can destroy.

The Eucharist is Resurrection food. If we consent to and co-operate with the Lord's action within us, then, over time, this flow of transforming energy from the Risen Lord into our lives frees what is still bound and releases a new capacity for generous love.

In the Eucharist, we are blessed that we might become a blessing for others, fed that we might be strong in goodness, filled that we might bear the fruit of Christ-like lives.

I am the living bread that came down from heaven. Whoever eats this bread will live forever. This bread is my flesh, which I will give for the life of the world ... Just as the living Father sent me and I live because of the Father, so the one who feeds on me will live because of me.

John 6:51, 57

✤✤✤✤✤

OUR SUSTAINING BREAD OF LIFE

Jesus, nourish my life
and enrich it with brave and
beautiful expressions of love.

Our friend
in divine mercy

✤

Mercy is the most beautiful face of God. Divine mercy reaches our broken world through the wounded heart of the Crucified Jesus. The heart of the Passion of Jesus was the passion in his heart for each of us. He, the sinless One, carried our sins, bore our wounds and died our death. He gave all that we might receive all. 'The thief crucified with Jesus asked him, "Jesus, remember me when you come into your kingdom." Jesus answered him, "Truly I tell you, today you will be with me in paradise"' (Luke 23:42–43). Jesus' tender promise to the 'good thief' speaks of how free the gift of his eternal love is.

The Lord alone can bring light out of our darkness, grace out of our sin and sorrow and shame, good out of our mess and failure.

'Come now, let us settle the matter,' says the Lord. *'Though your sins are like scarlet, they shall be as white as snow; though they are red as crimson, they shall be like wool.'*

Isaiah 1:18

Jesus constantly invites us to immerse ourselves in his divine mercy, and to leave the regrets of the past at the foot of his cross. Jesus knows only too well that there is no saint without a past and no sinner without a future!

✥✥✥✥✥

OUR FRIEND IN DIVINE MERCY

Jesus, flood my life with
your divine mercy. ✌

Our Lord

✦

Jesus came to them and said, 'All authority in heaven and on earth has been given to me ... And surely I am with you always, to the very end of the age'

(Matthew 28:18, 20).

The Risen Jesus has won the absolute victory over all death and darkness. As Lord of all, all authority has been given to him. We do not see that truth now, but one day we will see it in all its beauty and splendour.

To call Jesus our Lord means to acknowledge his loving authority over our lives. It means to enter into a relationship of trust with him, a commitment to listen to him and follow his way.

This idea might seem oppressive and stir up fear within us. However, surrender to Christ does not trap us, it frees us; it does not weaken but strengthens us. The ancient Christian saying states, 'To serve Christ is to reign.' When we bring our life under Jesus' loving authority and guidance we are never more free, never more our true selves. Guided by his Spirit, we are given back authority over our lives so that we are no longer driven by every mood and impulse.

Yielding to the Lord, acting on his word, and following him does not necessarily make life easy. It makes us strong enough to face life! There is nothing more blessed than a surrendered life in the hands of the Lord.

❖❖❖❖❖

OUR LORD

Jesus, my Lord, help me
to put aside doubt and fear and
let myself be guided by you. ❧

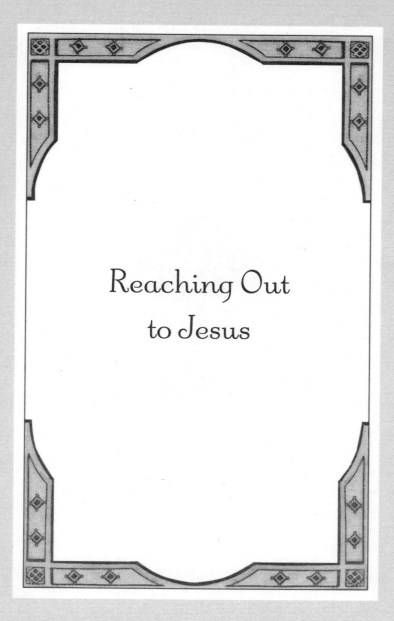

Reaching Out
to Jesus

Introduction

Everybody tried to touch him, because healing power went out from him, and he healed everyone.

Luke 6:19

When we call upon the name of Jesus in simple trust, we are reaching out to 'touch' him, just as truly as those people who reached out to him when he walked the lanes of Galilee. And we can have the experience of his compassion and healing power just as surely as they did. One of the simplest ways of reaching out to Jesus is to say his name in trust, but sometimes we have specific needs and wants. These reflections help us to reach out at all times, whatever our specific need.

The old hymn invites us:

Reach out and touch the Lord as he goes by.
You'll find he's not too busy to hear your heart's cry.
He's passing by this moment your needs to supply.
Reach out and touch the Lord as he goes by.

Whatever path we may be on, whatever our circumstances, Jesus journeys with us. He is listening for our heart's cry now. These simple reflections can be helpful in reaching out in trust to 'touch' Jesus.

We come to him with whatever faith we have – strong or fragile, convinced or feeble. In the presence of his absolute goodness, all we need is our need!

This is the simplest prayer, to call upon the name of Jesus and to reach out!

Everyone who calls on the name of the Lord will be saved.
Romans 10:13

May we experience the saving power that flows from the Lord!

When our faith is weak

Jesus asked the boy's father, 'How long has he been like this?'

'From childhood,' he answered. 'It has often thrown him into fire or water to kill him. But if you can do anything, take pity on us and help us.'

'If you can?' said Jesus. 'Everything is possible for one who believes.'

Immediately the boy's father exclaimed, 'I do believe, but help me overcome my unbelief!'

When Jesus saw that a crowd was running to the scene, he rebuked the impure spirit. 'You deaf and mute spirit,' he said. 'I command you, come out of him and never enter him again.'

The spirit shrieked, convulsed him violently and came out. The boy looked so much like a corpse that many said, 'He's dead.' But Jesus took him by the hand and lifted him to his feet, and he stood up.

Mark 9:22–24

The father of a terribly afflicted child brings his little boy to Jesus. In his desperate need, he cries out to the Lord to set his son free from his torment: 'If you can do anything, take pity on us'.

'If you can?' Jesus answers! The father's reply is wonderful. He is honest about both his belief and his unbelief. 'I do believe, but help me overcome my unbelief!'

That simple prayer is one that we can pray often and it goes straight to the Lord's heart.

We should be neither surprised nor upset with our doubts. Doubts and struggles in faith are normal stages of the spiritual journey. Doubts can rise up in us when it seems that our prayers are going unanswered and when we may feel abandoned in times of pain and suffering. God's grace is always at work in our lives even if at times it is difficult to believe this. Our prayers are answered according to our deepest needs.

We come to Jesus as we are now! We come, whatever our needs or weakness or our doubts. We can reach out to him no matter how our feeble our belief or how small our faith.

It may seem very inadequate to us but the Lord promises that if our faith is even the size of a mustard seed, he can work wonders with it. And in our very using of the little faith we do have to reach out to Jesus, our trust in him is increased.

WHEN OUR FAITH IS WEAK

Jesus, I do believe in you –
strengthen the little faith
I have; deepen my trust in you. ❧

When self-doubt limits us

Immediately Jesus made the disciples get into the boat and go on ahead of him to the other side, while he dismissed the crowd. After he had dismissed them, he went up on a mountainside by himself to pray. Later that night, he was there alone, and the boat was already a considerable distance from land, buffeted by the waves because the wind was against it.

Shortly before dawn Jesus went out to them, walking on the lake. When the disciples saw him walking on the lake, they were terrified. 'It's a ghost,' they said, and cried out in fear.

But Jesus immediately said to them, 'Take courage! It is I. Don't be afraid.'

'Lord, if it's you,' Peter replied, 'tell me to come to you on the water.'

'Come,' he said.

Then Peter got down out of the boat, walked on the water and came towards Jesus.

But when he saw the wind, he was afraid and, beginning to sink, cried out, 'Lord, save me!'

Immediately Jesus reached out his hand and caught him. 'You of little faith,' he said, 'why did you doubt?'

Matthew 14:22–31

Peter did walk on water! Yes, after a few steps he began to sink. But we can often forget that he began to walk on the water towards Jesus.

With his focus on Jesus and trusting in him, Peter got out of the boat. But when he felt the force of the wind, fear gripped him, he took his eyes off Jesus, doubted and started to sink.

How often do we not risk doing something new in our lives because of the doubts that rob us of hope? How often do they pull us back from change? Our doubts can limit and restrict us, trapping us in mediocrity.

The Lord invites us to step out of our self-imposed limitations, to keep our eyes fixed on him and do what our doubts say is impossible.

And at every step of the way, the Lord repeats to us, 'Take courage! It is I. Don't be afraid.'

WHEN SELF-DOUBT LIMITS US

Jesus, help me not to be
conquered by my doubts but
give me courage to move
into newness of life. ∿

When we are anxious

Are not five sparrows sold for two pennies? Yet not one of them is forgotten by God.

Indeed, the very hairs of your head are all numbered.

Don't be afraid; you are worth more than many sparrows.

Luke 12:6, 7

How often does Jesus have to tell us not to be afraid? How often does he have to invite us to trust in him?

There is no denying that our concerns can be real. However, we lose the balance of our souls when we allow anxiety to build up in us. It is like having our hand right in front of our face – it blocks the wider view.

If we believe we are never forgotten by God, that his love is so intimate that he numbers the very hairs on our heads, then we know the deepest things we need are not elsewhere.

The measure of our trust will be the measure of our peace. We can fully surrender our cares to the Lord only when we trust in his care for us.

The Word of God gives us clear guidance:

Do not be anxious about anything, but in every situation, by prayer and petition, with thanksgiving, present your requests to God. And the peace of God, which transcends all understanding, will guard your hearts and your minds in Christ Jesus.

Philippians 4:6, 7

WHEN WE ARE ANXIOUS

Jesus, I entrust all my cares
to you because I trust in
your care for me. ✍

When we seek interior healing

A man with leprosy came and knelt before him and said,
'Lord, if you are willing, you can make me clean.'

Jesus reached out his hand and touched the man.
'I am willing,' he said. 'Be clean!'

Immediately he was cleansed of his leprosy.

Matthew 8:2, 3

This poor man would have experienced nothing but rejection and contempt. Because people were so afraid of being infected, he would have been abandoned even by his own family.

And since his leprosy was seen as the result of his sin – anyone who had any contact with him became spiritually unclean. We can only imagine what inner torment he suffered. So Jesus' gentle touch not only healed his ravaged body but liberated his tortured soul.

It is the same for us as it was for that leper – Jesus is not only able to help us, he also wants to help us. 'I am willing.'

Whatever our physical needs may be, the Lord first looks to our heart. He sees deeper, to the wounds that we try to hide from others, from him and even from ourselves. Shame, self-rejection, fear, regret, resentment and bitterness can cripple us within.

The Lord cannot heal us of our deepest hurts unless we show him our wounds. He cannot break the chains that hold us captive unless we admit our bondage. It takes courage to show ourselves to Jesus as we really are. But what joy when his compassion touches the hidden depths and sets us free!

WHEN WE SEEK INTERIOR HEALING

Jesus, help me to show you
my wounds so you may touch
them with your tender and
liberating love. ꝰ

When our lives need to change

Jesus went into Galilee, proclaiming the good news of God.

'The time has come,' he said. 'The kingdom of God has come near. Repent and believe the good news!'

Mark 1:14–15

The call to repent can sound negative. But, in his love, Jesus is simply saying to us: Change the direction in which you are looking for happiness. Recognise where true joy can be found!

Prayer is one of the main ways Jesus brings this change about in our lives. He wants us to respond to the sometimes not so gentle 'nudges of the Spirit' given in prayer. His goodness draws us from self-reliance to God-reliance, from being ego-driven to Spirit-led. Grace loosens the hold that greed or selfishness or resentment or whatever else can have on our lives.

Change is never easy – we automatically resist leaving our comfort zones. So prayer not only shows us where we need to change, but assists us in our readiness to change. If we are persistently unwilling to change, then our prayer becomes superficial or is dropped altogether.

Prayer is not just talking; it is more than sweet feelings. Prayer is the first stage of surrender in trust to the Lord. True prayer leads us to move on from our self-centredness. It opens us to yield to grace, to allow ourselves to be guided by Jesus in our choices and decisions.

WHEN OUR LIVES NEED TO CHANGE

Jesus, I know you are calling
me to make some changes in
my life; give me both the desire and
the strength to follow
your leading. ✎

For help in our marriages

Some Pharisees came to him to test him. They asked, 'Is it lawful for a man to divorce his wife for any and every reason?'

'Haven't you read,' he replied, 'that at the beginning the Creator made them male and female and said, "For this reason a man will leave his father and mother and be united to his wife, and the two will become one flesh?"'

Matthew 19:3–5

Jesus teaches very clearly about the value and beauty of marriage. It is a God-given call to loving oneness, intimate companionship and mutual support.

However, married life, like all relationships, needs effort so that it can grow and deepen. Marriages go through different stages – some very difficult ones. Division and discord within marriage can be dreadfully painful. Those closest to us can hurt us most deeply precisely because what they say or do matters most to us.

It is good to pray frequently for our marriages, for the deepening of love and for the healing of hurts. Prayer takes the gracious presence of Jesus into our married lives so we can bear with one another's weaknesses and grow from each other's strengths.

We can be absolutely convinced that the Lord wants to protect and sustain our marriages. 'So they are no longer two, but one flesh. Therefore what God has joined together, let no one separate' (Matthew 19:6).

We can go to him with confidence when tension and disagreement increase. Harmony and cheerfulness within the home are a singular blessing.

FOR HELP IN OUR MARRIAGES

Jesus, bless our marriage,
our family and home; help us
to forgive one another's failings
and may the love that brought us
together be renewed and mature
with each passing year. ✎

For help in our relationships

*If you love those who love you, what credit is that to you?
Even sinners love those who love them. And if you do
good to those who are good to you, what credit is that to
you? Even sinners do that. And if you lend to those from
whom you expect repayment, what credit is that to you?
Even sinners lend to sinners, expecting to be repaid in full.*

*But love your enemies, do good to them and lend to them
without expecting to get anything back, then your reward*
will be great, and you will be children of the Most High,
because he is kind to the ungrateful and wicked.
Be merciful, just as your Father is merciful.*

Luke 6: 32–36

Our lives are made up of a network of relationships – family, relatives, friends, neighbours and work colleagues – there is no avoiding them! And there is no avoiding the hurt and conflict that at times can blight some of these relationships.

When such tensions arise, Jesus' guidance is very clear – our fundamental stance should be one of willingness to heal the rift and to be proactive in love. It is easy to be kind and helpful to those who return the favour. As those who have experienced God's merciful love in our own lives, Jesus asks more of us. As the saying goes, 'Where there is no love put love and then you will find love.' Even if the other person does not respond, we have done what we should do.

A real risk when we feel hurt and are angry with someone is that we begin to think about them obsessively, winning arguments in our heads and imagining what they are thinking or, even worse, saying about us. We talk about them to others and tell what they have done. All this reinforces the negativity and pushes the thorn of hurt deeper into our hearts where it can fester and seriously poison the relationship.

It is important at such times to guard the mind from obsessive thinking, close the mouth to bitter words and to take the actions of love.

The scriptures frequently come back to this important issue of the quality of our relationships.

But now you must also rid yourselves of all such things as these: anger, rage, malice, slander and filthy language from your lips ... Therefore, as God's chosen people, holy and dearly loved, clothe yourselves with compassion, kindness, humility, gentleness and patience. Bear with each other and forgive one another if any of you has a grievance against someone. Forgive as the Lord forgave you. And over all these virtues put on love, which binds them all together in perfect unity.

Colossians 3: 8, 12–14

FOR HELP IN OUR RELATIONSHIPS

Jesus, grant me the largeness
of heart to take the actions of love,
and to work to heal any wounds
in my relations with others. ◦

For our children

People were bringing little children to Jesus for him to place his hands on them, but the disciples rebuked them. When Jesus saw this, he was indignant.

He said to them, 'Let the little children come to me, and do not hinder them, for the kingdom of God belongs to such as these. Truly I tell you, anyone who will not receive the kingdom of God like a little child will never enter it.'

And he took the children in his arms, placed his hands on them and blessed them.

Mark 10:13–16

Jesus loved children and was only too happy to take them into his arms and bless them. Today, we too can bring our children to the Lord for his blessing. It is possible in heartfelt prayer to carry them, as it were, to Jesus and place them in his loving arms.

Whether aged three or thirty, our son or daughter is still our treasured child. And with our great love for them comes great concern that they be happy and protected from all danger.

When they are older, there can be immense sorrow in seeing them hurting and wounded by life. At times, they may lose their way, refuse to listen and take paths that we would not wish for them.

Then is the time to believe that our children are loved by Jesus even more than we love them and that they are always in his care.

As we pray, we can see, with the eyes of faith, Jesus place his hands on them and bless them.

FOR OUR CHILDREN

Jesus, I entrust my child to
your tender care and guidance.
I place him/her in the sheltering
of your love. ❧

When our conscience is troubled

But while he was still a long way off, his father saw him and was filled with compassion for him; he ran to his son, threw his arms around him and kissed him.

The son said to him, 'Father, I have sinned against heaven and against you. I am no longer worthy to be called your son.'

'But the father said to his servants, 'Quick! Bring the best robe and put it on him. Put a ring on his finger and sandals on his feet. Bring the fattened calf and kill it. Let's have a feast and celebrate. For this son of mine was dead and is alive again; he was lost and is found.' So they began to celebrate.

Luke 15:20–24

When Jesus told the parable of the prodigal son, he gave us a glimpse of the immense love that underpins our very existence.

Divine love waits to welcome, to forgive, to heal, to rejoice over us. Divine mercy runs to us and holds us in a warm embrace. Once a son always a son; once a daughter always a daughter!

No matter how great our sin, how far we have wandered, how delayed our return – it is never too late to turn to Jesus and confess our sin. Indeed, no matter how often we have to make the journey home to him, a joyous welcome awaits us. We can tire of asking for mercy but Jesus never tires of giving mercy.

Nothing is outside the scope of his unconditional love. His love has never been withdrawn – not even in our blackest, most bitter moments. We may feel that his pardon is too much to receive but it is never too much for him to give. We must not set limits to Jesus' mercy!

I have swept away your offences like a cloud, your sins like the morning mist. Return to me, for I have redeemed you.
Isaiah 44:22

What a joy to experience the power of merciful love!

WHEN OUR CONSCIENCE IS TROUBLED

Jesus, may I never doubt the depth
of your goodness; hold me in your
merciful embrace and grant me the
joy of a new beginning. ✍

When we seek spiritual energy

On the last and greatest day of the festival, Jesus stood and said in a loud voice, 'Let anyone who is thirsty come to me and drink. Whoever believes in me, as Scripture has said, rivers of living water will flow from within them.' By this he meant the Spirit, whom those who believed in him were later to receive.

John 7:37–39

The Risen Jesus is the fount of the Holy Spirit for us. His outpouring of his own divine life and energy into our lives is not something that is meant to happen just once. Jesus continually wishes to refresh us in the Spirit.

When our faith is feeble and we feel drained of the ability to pray, when we have no more capacity to live in love and in generosity of heart, then is the time to ask Jesus for a fresh, lavish outpouring of his Spirit.

The strength of the Holy Spirit is for our day-to-day living. It is in daily life that we need the energy, grace, courage, patience, insight, wisdom and love that are the fruit of the presence of the Spirit within us.

The Holy Spirit is gifted to us not in a vague, general way. The graces and help given are suited uniquely to each person's life and situation. The Spirit's divine action is tailored according to our particular needs at different stages of our life.

So what are the relationships, responsibilities and struggles in our life now? Where the providence of God has led us, there the Spirit of God is available to us.

So the Lord invites us today, 'If you are thirsty, come. If you believe, drink.'

WHEN WE SEEK SPIRITUAL ENERGY

Jesus, I thirst for a new
outpouring of your Spirit now;
I come to you in faith
to drink my fill! ∂

In addiction

*In the synagogue, there was a man possessed by a demon,
an impure spirit. He cried out at the top of his voice,
'Go away! What do you want with us, Jesus of Nazareth?
Have you come to destroy us? I know who you are –
the Holy One of God!'*

'Be quiet!' Jesus said sternly. 'Come out of him!'

*Then the demon threw the man down before them all
and came out without injuring him.*

Luke 4:33–35

Again and again, Jesus shows that he has authority over the powers of darkness and all that would hold us in slavery.

Many things in our lives can become addictive, linked with obsessive thinking and compulsive behaviour. Then we can experience the chaos of being out of control. This is a form of spiritual bondage.

At the moment of temptation, when we feel helpless before its fierce strength, we cry out in Jesus' name for freedom. 'Salvation is found in no one else, for there is no other name under heaven given to mankind by which we must be saved' (Acts 4:12).

We bring our struggle into the light of his presence and his authority. We let our very powerlessness open us to the Lord's power and carry us to God.

He reached down from on high and took hold of me; he drew me out of deep waters. He rescued me from my powerful enemy, from my foes, who were too strong for me. They confronted me in the day of my disaster, but the Lord was my support. He brought me out into a spacious place; he rescued me because he delighted in me.

Psalms 18:16–19

IN ADDICTION

Jesus, I am powerless
over this addictive behaviour
but you are not; in your
unfailing love set me free. ✍

In depression

At noon, darkness came over the whole land until three in the afternoon. And at three in the afternoon, Jesus cried out in a loud voice, 'Eloi, Eloi, lema sabachthani?' (which means 'My God, my God, why have you forsaken me?').

Mark 15:33, 34

With unimaginable love, Jesus willingly experienced on the cross the crushing weight of our sin and shame, and all the pain and sorrow of our broken lives so that we might be free of them. This included the sense of utter desolation, of feeling abandoned even by God. And so his heartfelt cry to his heavenly Father.

There can be times in our lives also when the dark descends and we are trapped in our loneliness and confusion. At these times, it can appear that the darkness is total, God has forgotten us and our life has no hope or purpose. There are few sufferings as awful as this black despair.

Yet even then, in sheer faith, we can reach out to open ourselves to the divine energy that flows from the Risen Jesus. In our mental anguish, to simply say over and over 'Jesus mercy' can bring even a glimmer of hope. We can find the grace to let him love us through the care of family and friends.

We know that Jesus' last words on the cross were a prayer of childlike trust: 'Father, into your hands I commit my spirit' (Luke 23:46). With him, we put our soul into the Father's hands that he may revive what is dead in us. We pray to be released from the grip of our own mind, to be protected from our own frenzied thinking.

May Christ be the light which dispels our darkness and restores calm to our inner chaos.

IN DEPRESSION

Jesus, be a light in my
darkness; let me know you
have not abandoned me. ♫

In need of protection

How often I have longed to gather your children together, as a hen gathers her chicks under her wings, and you were not willing.

Luke 13:34

Jesus lamented over Jerusalem because its people refused his gift of love. Today in his tender care for us, Jesus offers us his presence as a shield, as chicks hide under the mother-hen's wings in time of danger. But we too, in our stubborn self-will, can pull back from his embrace.

A shelter is of little value unless we take cover under its protection; a refuge is of no use unless we run to it for safety.

There are times when the dangers that threaten us are clear, whether of body, mind or soul. At such times, we can take the Lord at his word and shelter in the security of his loving presence.

Then we can pray with confidence in his abiding promise:

I call on you, my God, for you will answer me; turn your ear to me and hear my prayer. Show me the wonders of your great love, you who save by your right hand those who take refuge in you from their foes. Keep me as the apple of your eye; hide me in the shadow of your wings.

Psalms 17:6–8

In need of protection

Jesus, I know I sometimes
refuse to come to you for refuge;
now I seek shelter under
your protecting love. ❧

Needing peace of heart

I have told you these things, so that in me you may have peace. In this world you will have trouble. But take heart! I have overcome the world.

John 16:33

At the Last Supper, Jesus tells his disciples of unavoidable troubles ahead. But he also promises them his peace no matter what difficulties they may face.

The Lord frequently speaks of life's struggles. In doing so, he is simply being real. Life is fragile and, at times, the road ahead can be steep and hard and lonely. Sorrow and loss of whatever sort and for whatever reason pierce every soul at some time.

Jesus wants us to understand that any vision of life, any spirituality that does not take into account the reality of suffering and pain, is of little use to us. His message is not about running from our troubles but of peace in the midst of troubles.

Jesus encourages us to 'take heart' and to draw courage from his victory, a victory he wants to share with us now. This is the source of our deep peace – a peace that can be deeper than any surface turmoil.

He will never leave us and his promise of peace stands forever. 'Peace I leave with you; my peace I give you. I do not give to you as the world gives. Do not let your hearts be troubled and do not be afraid' (John 14:27).

NEEDING PEACE OF HEART

Jesus, no matter what
my troubles, don't let me
lose the peace you want
me to have. ❧

In need of comfort

Blessed are those who mourn, for they will be comforted.

Matthew 5:4

In this Beatitude, Jesus promises us comfort when heartbreak of whatever sort threatens to shatter us. This divine comfort not only consoles us but also protects us from any bitterness that might take root in our hearts — bitterness against life, others or God.

We need this grace because the heart can break in different ways. It can break in a way that softens, cleanses and opens it in compassion and generosity to others. Or it can break in a way that makes it sour, hard and cold, closing us off from others. Heartbreaks can be warm or cold.

It is the way suffering is faced that makes the difference — whether it stretches or shrinks the soul, blesses or burns, makes us better or bitter!

When the harshness of life strips us, how do we live so that we do not become embittered?

When sorrow comes to us, it is crucial that we go in our pain and need to Jesus. We do not close ourselves off from the very one who can console and sustain us. We come to him just as we are and pour out our hearts before him — all that they may carry. We tell him as it is!

In the very act of honestly opening ourselves to him, we are also opening ourselves to his comfort and support.

IN NEED OF COMFORT

Jesus, in times of sorrow,
comfort me and guard my
heart from bitterness. ✍

When seeking rest for our souls

Come to me, all you who are weary and burdened, and I will give you rest. Take my yoke upon you and learn from me, for I am gentle and humble in heart, and you will find rest for your souls.

Matthew 11:28–30

This is probably Jesus' most treasured promise. He invites us, tired and burdened, to come and rest in him so that we can then continue refreshed on our journey with him.

We need this soul rest constantly because the pains of life, the losses we undergo, are either transmitted or transformed. If they are not transformed through humble acceptance of reality and surrendering in loving trust, then we transmit them – then the pain and hurt can flow into our attitudes and relationships. It all can come out in hypersensitivity, sarcasm, anger, resentments, living trapped in the past, or in words that wound and tear down. Hurt people hurt people!

This promise of Jesus is for us whenever we want to be rid of the load we struggle under and cannot be free of. The way to receive what he is offering is to come with child-like trust before the Lord and to open ourselves at a deep level to his gentle, humble love – this is what gives rest to our souls, eases the pain of life and protects us from passing on the pain.

WHEN SEEKING REST FOR OUR SOULS

Jesus, I come to you now
to find the rest you promise me;
help me to bring you my hurts and
not to transmit them to others. ∾

When we are battered by life's storms

Leaving the crowd behind, they took him along, just as he was, in the boat. There were also other boats with him. A furious squall came up, and the waves broke over the boat, so that it was nearly swamped.

Jesus was in the stern, sleeping on a cushion. The disciples woke him and said to him, 'Teacher, don't you care if we drown?'

He got up, rebuked the wind and said to the waves, 'Quiet! Be still!' Then the wind died down and it was completely calm.

He said to his disciples, 'Why are you so afraid? Do you still have no faith?'

Mark 4:36–40

Like the disciples caught in the storm, when fear takes hold of us, it can master us completely. Then our panic can spin out of control.

And worse still – it seems Jesus is uninterested, even asleep! So we can feel like crying out, 'Don't you care? I'm sinking here!'

Whatever about the problems we are facing, Jesus first has to calm the inner turmoil that fear has stirred up. He needs to tell the storms in our hearts, 'Quiet! Be still!'

Jesus knows that in the squalls of life we can be so swamped by panic that we become blind to his presence and so forget to trust. Losing sight of his goodness and strength in our fear, we feel powerless and defeated.

He asks us to let him replace fear with faith. Simple trust in him releases his saving love into every situation.

WHEN WE ARE BATTERED BY
LIFE'S STORMS

Jesus, when fear grips me,
still my soul and turn my heart
towards you in faith. ✑

In times of discontent

At that time Jesus, full of joy through the Holy Spirit, said, 'I praise you, Father, Lord of heaven and earth, because you have hidden these things from the wise and learned, and revealed them to little children.

Luke 10:21

The pages of the Bible are soaked with the language of thanksgiving. Here, we see Jesus giving heartfelt gratitude to his heavenly Father for how God is working through Jesus' ministry.

The spirit of discontent is the opposite of gratitude. This soul sickness can rob lives of peace and drain homes of happiness. This happens when we get into the habit of unfavourably contrasting our lives with those of other people.

Then, the seed of discontent is able to put down roots in our hearts. The spirit of niggling fault-finding grows and grows until we become embittered with our situation. Such discontent makes us miserable and a misery to be around.

There is no such thing as the perfect family, the perfect marriage, the perfect job or the perfect circumstances in life. But nor is there any life without reasons for gratitude.

The root of discontent is not the lack of blessings in our lives; it is being inattentive to those blessings. Gratitude works like a vaccine to keep us from being infected with a spirit of discontent. We open ourselves to what is called 'the grace of enoughness'!

Awareness of our blessings connects us with God. Are we blessing-conscious or problem-conscious? Jesus invites us to count our blessings, not our problems.

IN TIMES OF DISCONTENT

Jesus, help me not to
trudge through my days
and be blind to the blessings
that surround me. ✍

In appreciating creation

Look at the birds of the air; they do not sow or reap or store away in barns, and yet your heavenly Father feeds them. Are you not much more valuable than they? ... See how the flowers of the field grow. They do not labour or spin. Yet I tell you that not even Solomon in all his splendour was dressed like one of these.

Matthew 6:26, 28–29

It is obvious that Jesus loved to ponder the beauty and richness of nature that surrounded him. Very many of his teachings and parables speak of what he saw in the fields and skies.

St Francis also drew great joy and inspiration from spending time in nature. In his great 'Canticle of the Creatures', he delighted in Brother Sun, Sister Moon, our Sister Mother Earth, and in fire, water and wind. All spoke to him of the Creator; all mirrored divine goodness. From the Franciscan perspective, the world is pregnant with God!

It is good to celebrate the gift of creation in a spirit of wonder and thanksgiving. It is important for us to cease the hectic rushing – even briefly – to simply notice the world around us, teeming with life and colour and extraordinary diversity.

To pause and relish a blackbird's song or to find delight in a humble primrose, these too are moments of grace, of spiritual refreshment.

Jesus tells us simply, 'Look at the birds ... See the flowers.'

In appreciating creation

Jesus, open my eyes to
rejoice in the beauty and
goodness of God's creation. ℘

When needing to forgive (1)

Do not judge, and you will not be judged.
Do not condemn, and you will not be condemned.
Forgive, and you will be forgiven.

Luke 6:37

Very many of us carry hurts and resentments from the past – from childhood, family and previous relationships or from injustices done to us.

Sometimes, this resentment can be a palpable, constant presence. Other times, resentments are denied because these memories and emotions are so hard to face. But just because something is covered does not mean it is healed. Just because something is denied does not mean it is not influencing our daily living. Just because someone is dead does not mean the hurt is dead.

As we grow in our friendship with the Lord, there comes a time when the burdens of hurt and anger carried from the past need to be named and, by God's grace, put down in forgiveness.

It is a law of life, hard but true, that when a deep injury has been done to us, we do not find healing and peace until we forgive. Revenge has never yet healed a wound.

The first step to freedom is simply to acknowledge the resentment, to bring it into the light before the Lord, and to ask for the strength to put it down. Jesus, who prayed on the cross for those who were killing him, will give us the strength to let go, if we seek it from him. We give our hurt to the Lord as often as we must and ask for the healing of our own soul.

WHEN NEEDING TO FORGIVE (1)

Jesus, help me to be honest
about the resentments I carry;
give me the courage to
begin to let them go. ❧

When needing to forgive (2)

But love your enemies, do good to them, and lend to them without expecting to get anything back. Then your reward will be great, and you will be children of the Most High, because he is kind to the ungrateful and wicked. Be merciful, just as your Father is merciful.

Luke 6:35, 36

One of Jesus' most constant teachings is about forgiveness. Again and again, he comes back to the necessity of cleansing our hearts of all resentment, bitterness and of the desire for revenge.

He asks us to forgive because he loves us. He knows what damage the refusal to forgive does to us.

Resentment is an acid that destroys its container and the container is our own heart! Resentment keeps hurts alive in our souls, controls our moods and extends our pain. It can grow like a cancer poisoning our very selves.

We are being very good to ourselves when we make the decision to let go of any bitterness we are nursing. To be able to put down the burdens of past resentments is always a precious gift.

The way before us is steep enough without carrying the terrible load of our hurts and grudges. Jesus asks us not to carry into the future what he wants us to put down, to lay aside now.

Without forgiveness we simply cannot move forward. But with forgiveness, we are freed from the cold grip of the past. Forgiveness is medicine for our hearts. In forgiving, we regain our souls.

WHEN NEEDING TO FORGIVE (2)

Jesus, help me to see that
your love wants me free of
bitterness and your grace
can do it. ✒

When needing to forgive (3)

But to you who are listening I say, 'Love your enemies, do good to those who hate you, bless those who curse you, pray for those who mistreat you.'

Luke 6:27, 28

Jesus is not asking the impossible when he asks us to forgive. His grace helps us to put down the heavy burden of the past, to stop picking at the scab of our injury.

Loving our enemies does not mean pretending that nothing ever happened or that we have forgotten. It does not mean pretending to have warm feelings for them. It means we wish them well, not evil. And Jesus tells us what brings about this change of heart: 'Pray for those who mistreat you.' He knows it is very hard to continue resenting a person you are praying for.

It is important that we understand that we don't have to like someone before we pray for them. Nor do we have to wait until our emotions are no longer raw before doing so. We can simply say, whenever the bitter memory surfaces, 'Lord, I no longer want to carry this. Bless him/her and grant me peace!'

Feelings follow the action. Forgiveness is not firstly about our emotions; it is a choice, a decision, an act of the will. Such a choosing of forgiveness in simple prayer opens space within for the Lord to bring us healing and peace.

If the wound is deep, we may need to make that choice again and again until our heart is free.

For our own good, we constantly put it all in Jesus' hands, and in time, divine compassion goes deep!

WHEN NEEDING TO FORGIVE (3)

Jesus, I choose to forgive
and I pray now for all those
who have treated me badly. ✑

When angry with the Lord

On his arrival, Jesus found that Lazarus had already been in the tomb for four days ... When Martha heard that Jesus was coming, she went out to meet him, but Mary stayed at home.

'Lord,' Martha said to Jesus, 'if you had been here, my brother would not have died. But I know that even now God will give you whatever you ask.'

John 11:17, 20–22

Martha and Mary had sent for Jesus when their brother was seriously sick. The Lord did not come immediately, and Lazarus died. We can hear in Martha's words a rebuke of Jesus for his delay in coming.

We might not voice our own rebukes in prayer, but our hearts can feel them. When prayers seem unanswered, feeling let down by the Lord when hurt by life, or the sense of his absence – all these things can lead to harboured anger against the Lord. We can blame him even without realising it.

These feelings, if not acknowledged, weaken trust. Doubt in Jesus' love and his real care for us can take root. Defences can form within us that unknowingly resist the divine goodness. These can lodge in the heart and filter out the love being offered to us.

When this happens, Jesus' mercy has to heal our hearts. Then, the change we need is not so much about our ideas about the Lord, but how we feel about him! We begin by being honest and telling Jesus what we are really feeling.

Later, before bringing her brother back to life, Jesus would say to Martha, 'Did I not tell you that you would see God's glory if you believe?' (John 11:40). Our lives are in God's hands – strong, loving and safe – we can trust him even when it seems that he has forgotten us.

WHEN ANGRY WITH THE LORD

Jesus, I do not always
understand how you are
at work in my life; replace any
resistance to your love with
an ever deeper trust in you. ◇

In thanks for our friends

Some men came carrying a paralysed man on a mat and tried to take him into the house to lay him before Jesus. When they could not find a way to do this because of the crowd, they went up on the roof and lowered him on his mat through the tiles into the middle of the crowd, right in front of Jesus.

When Jesus saw their faith, he said, 'Friend, your sins are forgiven ... Which is easier: to say, "Your sins are forgiven" or to say, "Get up and walk"? But I want you to know that the Son of Man has authority on earth to forgive sins.' So he said to the paralysed man, 'I tell you, get up, take your mat and go home.'

Immediately, he stood up in front of them, took what he had been lying on and went home praising God.

Luke 5:18–20, 23–25

That man had very good friends. They not only carried him to Jesus but then made every effort to bring him to Jesus' attention. Their love for their friend and their faith in the Lord worked. The man went home dancing for joy – healed in body and soul!

There are people in our lives who have carried us to Jesus. Indeed, even today, there may be those who are taking us – in prayer – before the divine presence.

How many times have we been supported in loving kindness, sustained in faith by a simple word, encouraged by good example, prayed for – even unknown to ourselves?

These are the Lord's blessings coming to us through others. This is how we are carried towards healing and hope when by ourselves we cannot meet the challenge of the hour. Then we lean into the faith of others.

To be able to recognise these life-giving gestures in our lives is a gift. And we in turn are invited to help others on their path.

IN THANKS FOR OUR FRIENDS

Jesus, I thank you for those
who, with great love, have brought
me to you. Help me also to support
others on their journey of grace. ✍

When seeking guidance on life's journey

I am the light of the world. Whoever follows me will never walk in darkness, but will have the light of life.

John 8:12

Jesus makes a wonderful promise – we will walk in the light of life. The proviso, before that blessing can be realised for us, is that we follow him. The invitation is to walk, step by step, after the Lord.

There are times when we come to a crossroads in life's journey. There are decisions to be made and various choices before us. The path ahead may be far from certain.

Then we go to the Lord in simple prayer and seek his guidance. When we turn to the source of all wisdom, we will make fewer unwise choices. In whatever choice we make, we choose to act with integrity.

This involves not rushing into a decision. We want to align our lives with Jesus' purpose for us and this may mean waiting until the Lord's will is made clear to us.

There are times when all we can do is ask and trust and wait! This waiting is not lost time. When we wait in humble trust for the Lord's guidance, his grace is powerfully at work in our lives.

In the light of his presence, our lives unfold according to his love and timing.

WHEN SEEKING GUIDANCE ON
LIFE'S JOURNEY

Jesus, show me your ways,
guide me and lead me, for you
are the light for my path. ∾

In times of letting go

Very truly I tell you, unless a kernel of wheat falls to the ground and dies, it remains only a single seed. But if it dies, it produces many seeds.

John 12:24

Jesus was speaking shortly before his own death – a dying in total love that would bring life to the world.

The grain falls into the dark earth – all seems lost – but new life and fruitfulness come from that very dying. This rhythm of nature is also the pattern of our own lives. This dying in order to rise, this letting go so that newness may come is something we cannot avoid no matter how hard we try.

There is a time for being born and a time for dying – and there are many dyings and rebirths in our lives.

We can attempt to cling on to something whose time has come. It may be a relationship, a job, a place, our status – the list is endless. If we do, we delay the next stage of our life and we hinder growth because we don't let go.

It is time to let go, to move on. We need to grieve what was important, even precious, to us and let it fall gently away. Release what needs to be released. Accept what needs to be accepted.

Then we can be open to receive gifts, as yet unimagined.

IN TIMES OF LETTING GO

Jesus, it is so painful for me
to let go; help me to surrender
so that I move into the
future in freedom. ❧

With a grateful heart

Six days before the Passover, Jesus came to Bethany, where Lazarus lived, whom Jesus had raised from the dead. Here a dinner was given in Jesus' honour. Martha served, while Lazarus was among those reclining at the table with him.

Then Mary took about a pint of pure nard, an expensive perfume; she poured it on Jesus' feet and wiped his feet with her hair. And the house was filled with the fragrance of the perfume.

John 12:1–3

The heart of Mary, the sister of Martha and Lazarus, overflowed with thankfulness. A few days earlier, Jesus had restored Lazarus to life. So she poured out the costly perfume as an intimate gesture of her love and gratitude.

It is wonderful to experience a canticle of joyful gratitude rise up in our hearts. And we all have so much to be grateful for. Every breath each of us takes is the direct personal gift of life given to us by God our Creator. Divine love has created us, mercy has rescued us, providence has provided for us and wisdom has guided our steps.

No matter what is going on in our lives now — there are always grounds for gratitude. Often we may need to pray to be aware of how Jesus' unceasing kindness comes to us through many ordinary people and situations.

When we identify the signs of the Lord's gracious goodness to us, a sense of thankfulness pervades our lives like a beautiful fragrance. The grateful heart is a happy heart.

I will give thanks to you, Lord, with all my heart; I will tell of all your wonderful deeds. I will be glad and rejoice in you; I will sing the praises of your name, O Most High.

Psalms 9:1, 2

WITH A GRATEFUL HEART

Jesus, give me a heart that
is warmed by gratitude,
a heart that pours out a
canticle of thanksgiving. ❧

When we are burdened by shame

Then seizing Jesus, they led him away and took him into the house of the high priest. Peter followed at a distance. And when some there had kindled a fire in the middle of the courtyard and had sat down together, Peter sat down with them.

A servant girl saw him seated there in the firelight. She looked closely at him and said, 'This man was with him.'

But he denied it. 'Woman, I don't know him,' he said.

A little later someone else saw him and said, 'You also are one of them.'

'Man, I am not!' Peter replied.

About an hour later another asserted, 'Certainly this fellow was with him, for he is a Galilean.'

Peter replied, 'Man, I don't know what you're talking about!'

Just as he was speaking, the rooster crowed. The Lord turned and looked straight at Peter. Then Peter remembered the word the Lord had spoken to him: 'Before the rooster crows today, you will disown me three times.' And he went outside and wept bitterly.

Luke 22:54–62

Peter failed, and failed grievously – he denied his Lord, his friend. After that experience, he might have spent a stunted life, never escaping from the shame of what he had done. But the Risen Jesus restored Peter in love, and helped him to lay aside the terrible weight of his betrayal.

Some of us can drag the past behind us like a ball and chain, burdened by a sense of sin. We can never let go of our failures, of actions we now regret, or of hurt we have caused others.

Not liking ourselves, we imagine God does not like us. So we find it hard to pray, to experience any peace of soul. Wounded by crippling shame, we cannot accept the Lord's forgiveness and we will not forgive ourselves. The past controls our lives.

Jesus asks us to make our amends for the past, as best we can. He then invites us to bring the crushing burden of our remorse and regret to his cross and leave it there. We have carried it far too long. His saving grace does not depend on what we have done but rather on what he has done for us. Grace is free only because Jesus himself has borne the full cost.

Now, by his love, we can stop listening to our inner voice that speaks cruel, unforgiving words. We liberate ourselves from our own harsh judgement, release ourselves from the bondage of our own self-condemnation.

In the experience of unearned, absolute love, we take our toxic shame and throw it away.

WHEN WE ARE BURDENED BY SHAME

Jesus, I bring all my failures
and regrets to your cross;
in your merciful love gift me
with a new beginning. ✏

In compassion for others

Now Thomas (also known as Didymus), one of the Twelve, was not with the disciples when Jesus came. So the other disciples told him, 'We have seen the Lord!'

But he said to them, 'Unless I see the nail marks in his hands and put my finger where the nails were, and put my hand into his side, I will not believe.'

A week later, his disciples were in the house again and Thomas was with them. Though the doors were locked, Jesus came and stood among them and said, 'Peace be with you!' Then he said to Thomas, 'Put your finger here; see my hands. Reach out your hand and put it into my side. Stop doubting and believe.'

Thomas said to him, 'My Lord and my God!'

John 20:24–28

What an extraordinary image! Thomas reaches out tentatively, fearfully and touches the Lord's wounds – the wounds of his love for us that the Risen Jesus will bear forever. And touching the Lord's wounds heals Thomas' own wounds of doubt and unbelief. 'My Lord and my God': this is the strongest act of faith in who Jesus is that is found anywhere in the entire Bible.

This dynamic – touching the Lord's wounds so our wounds are healed – is a reality that still abides. For us also, touching the Lord's wounds opens us to deeper faith and love.

But how do we reach out and make contact with his wounds? We touch the wounds of Jesus when we touch the brokenness of his suffering body. In the profound mystery of our oneness with the Risen Lord, our wounds are the wounds of the body of Christ. Jesus said, 'I tell you the truth, whatever you did for the least of these brothers of mine, you did for me' (Matthew 25:40).

When we touch with compassion the suffering members of Christ's body, we are touching the Lord's wounds. And when we open our hearts to give, to give in loving kindness in whatever way, we also are opening ourselves to receive – to receive from the Lord grace and light.

We grow in deeper faith and in intimacy with Jesus when we take our eyes off ourselves and show love to our wounded brothers and sisters. Touching his wounds still brings blessings!

IN COMPASSION FOR OTHERS

Jesus, help me to touch
you in those who need my love
and compassion this day. ⤸

In any need

*And a woman was there who had been subject to bleeding
for twelve years. She had suffered a great deal under the care
of many doctors and had spent all she had, and yet instead
of getting better, she grew worse.* When she heard about
Jesus, she came up behind him in the crowd and touched his
cloak, because she thought, If I just touch his clothes, I will
be healed. *Immediately, her bleeding stopped and she felt
in her body that she was freed from her suffering.*

*At once Jesus realised that power had gone out from him.
He turned around in the crowd and asked, 'Who touched
my clothes?'*

*'You see the people crowding against you,' his disciples
answered, 'and yet you can ask, "Who touched me?"'*

*But Jesus kept looking around to see who had done it.
Then the woman, knowing what had happened to her,
came and fell at his feet and, trembling with fear, told
him the whole truth.*

*He said to her, 'Daughter, your faith has healed you.
Go in peace and be freed from your suffering.'*

Mark 5:25–34

This good woman teaches us the power of touching Jesus in faith. Many in the crowd were bumping into Jesus. Only one person reached out intentionally and made contact with him in expectant faith. 'If I just touch his clothes, I will be healed.' And Jesus knew the difference instantly. Our trust in him gets his attention every time.

The person who believes in Jesus touches Jesus! Our faith puts us into true contact with the Living Lord, opens us to his love and releases his power in our lives.

The woman was so fearful about touching Jesus because the bleeding she suffered from made her ritually 'unclean' according to the Jewish law. And according to that law anyone who made contact with her would also be rendered 'unclean'. But instead of shrinking back, in her desperate need, she reached out in faith. And like a surge of warm energy, she felt the Lord's strength and healing fill her body.

We must never allow fear or shame keep us from approaching Jesus. He is waiting for us to reach out and touch him.

IN ANY NEED

Jesus, help me to reach
out to you in hope, to touch
you in faith, and to receive
from you with great joy. ♄

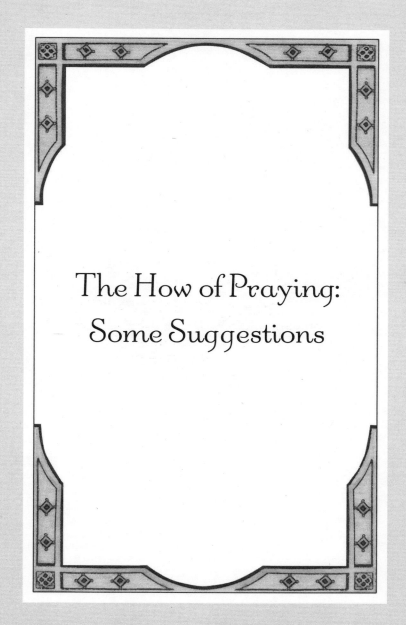

The How of Praying:
Some Suggestions

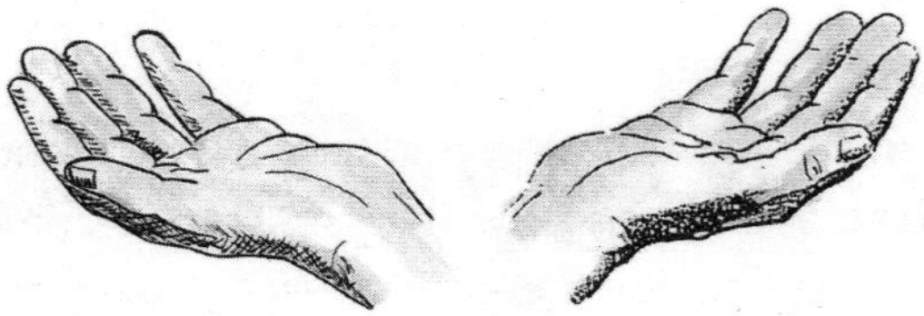

Introduction

❖

Like an apple tree with roots deep in the soil, standing in the sunshine and watered by the rain, so we come before the Lord letting his love feed us, warm us and make us grow. In prayer, we are letting him love us into life, freedom and fruitfulness.

When we pray, we are invited to trust his love, not to dismiss it as too good to be true, and not to reject it because of a sense of our own unworthiness. Jesus loves us first – all the time.

No matter what is going on in our lives – marriage or family struggles, financial issues, habitual patterns of sin, bereavement, remorse about the past or fear about what lies ahead – Jesus asks us to open ourselves in prayer and to allow

133

his light pierce our darkness, his power touch our weakness and his life revive our heaviness of spirit.

In this section, we look at some practical suggestions that may help us to be more open to his healing touch.

We need not worry about making mistakes in praying. We pray as best we can and it is always pleasing to the Lord. What matters is that we do pray. And the more we pray, the more prayer transforms us.

Slowing down

Prayer is oxygen for the soul. Just as the body needs to breathe, so we need to allow our souls to draw in deeply the love that is the very source of our existence.

Often, we bring to prayer the hectic pace that can pervade our days. And then we can wonder why there was no awareness of the Lord's presence. Many blessings of consolation and guidance and encouragement are not received because the vessel of our heart is already filled, busy about many things.

So, rather than rushing into prayer, it is good to change pace and prepare our hearts. We slow down, find some solitude, move into silence, and still the mind and heart. 'When you pray, go into your room, close the door and pray to your Father, who is unseen' (Matthew 6:6). We consciously enter into our inner sanctuary. A sacred space can greatly help. For some of us, it may be a corner of a room with a comfortable chair and a crucifix and Bible on a table, for others it may be a quiet spot at the back of a church we pass daily on the way to work.

There is a power in simple rituals to help us centre the heart and mind. Some of us may light a candle before an icon or cross. Others of us may bless ourselves slowly and prayerfully, invoking the Spirit to lead us in prayer.

We bring our bodies to prayer. If we notice that we are carrying tension in our bodies, we can sit straight and breathe in slowly and gently, holding our breath briefly before exhaling. Doing this several times can help ease stress and calm the body. All of this is both a preparation for prayer and a prayer itself.

The image of our heart as an open vessel, ready to receive, has been used to describe the interior disposition that most blesses us in prayer. We take time to prepare our heart so that we come before the Lord receptive and docile to his grace.

A powerful prayer of trust that gives the Lord freedom in our prayer might be: 'Jesus, all that you want to give me, I long to receive. All that you long to do in me, with all my heart I want it to happen.'

Rhythms for life

The notion of habit when speaking of our prayer can seem strange. We can feel that our relationship with the Lord should be spontaneous. And, indeed, mindless routine is not what we aim for! The terms 'rhythms' or 'patterns' are probably more suitable. If we are to be realistic about growing in prayer, we need a rhythm or pattern to our daily lives that supports that prayer. We build into our days what nourishes our soul.

A key rhythm is time set aside each day to spend with the Lord. All relationships require time to grow. Our relationship with Jesus is no different. We are busy and we do not have time for everything. In the end, we make time for the things we believe are really important. Choices have to be made. Nothing shapes our lives more than the commitments we choose. The fundamental question for us is who or what gets our commitment? It is a sobering thought that we are as close to the Lord as we choose to be. His love for us does not waver. But the extent to which that love enters and impacts on our lives depends on our free choices.

Our spiritual well-being and growth are very practical matters. Scriptures often compare training for the Christian life to the way athletes stay in shape. 'Train yourself to be godly. For physical training is of some value, but godliness has value for all things, holding promise for both the present life, here and the life to come' (1 Timothy 4:7, 8).

We cannot manufacture or force grace. God is free and his self-giving to us in love is always pure gift. But we can dispose ourselves to be open and receptive. The surfer cannot create the wave. But if he wants to surf, he has to get into the water and be prepared to ride the wave when it comes. We foster a rhythm in our daily lives that keeps us ready and available for the wave of the Spirit!

The desire of the heart

Be still, and know that I am God.

Psalms 46:10

The idea of being still before the Lord can be very attractive. But when we try to quieten down in his presence, our minds can run riot. Incessant distractions can keep us from focusing on our prayer. It is comforting to know that this is normal for most of us.

A helpful distinction is to recognise the difference between intention and attention in our prayer. Our intention to pray, the desire of the heart, is what is essential. Our attention in prayer will always waver, more or less. Jesus looks to the heart – the desire to pray *is* prayer in his eyes!

We might begin by saying, 'Lord, I want to spend this time with you. This is the desire, the intention of my heart. Even if my mind wanders the world over, may my heart be fixed on you.'

Then we simply keep returning, as often as we become aware of our wandering mind, to the divine presence. We come back gently. It can be very helpful to have a prayer word or phrase – 'Jesus', 'Abba Father' or 'Come, Holy Spirit' – that we use peacefully to refocus the heart. We let the distraction go without strain. If we get upset with our endless stream of thoughts and images, we only strengthen them.

If we want to pray, we are praying – no matter how chaotic our thoughts. We do not try to judge our success or failure in prayer, we simply turn up faithfully and humbly give to the Lord what we can offer. The benefits of prayer are experienced most often not at the time of prayer, but in daily living.

At times, our muddled efforts can seem futile to us, even a waste of time, but there is a deeper reality of grace and love at work in our prayer than we can ever understand.

Living in the now

Many of us can live our lives crucified between two thieves: regret about the past and anxiety about the future. These 'thieves' rob us of truly living in the present moment, the only time we have. They deprive us of peace of heart, and also of authentic prayer and friendship with the Lord.

For God is always in the now. He wants us to leave the past to his compassion. And to trust that his presence will be there for us whatever lies ahead. But it is in the details of today where the Lord's love is active.

God comes to us disguised as our lives. Jesus is in the facts of our lives today. Genuine prayer comes from and reflects our daily living. Our life now is the raw material of our relationship with the Lord, of our growth in holiness.

If this is so, then we need to remain alert to the present moment to recognise him. Staying in the now, we stay in contact with the Lord. Every day we can reach out to 'touch' him a hundred times, bringing ourselves back to the present and to his presence. A gentle movement of the heart puts us in touch with the fullness of his love and grace.

A whispered thanks when blessings are recognised. The name of Jesus called upon during a pause in work, when stopped in the traffic or at times of stress. His presence invoked when tensions rise in relationships, for the strength to hold back the angry word or to forget the self in deeds of love.

Nothing in our lives is too large for his power, nothing is too small for his loving concern. But it is only in the now that we can reach out to him, and only in the present moment can his grace be set free in our lives.

Honest to God

The psalmist encourages us: 'Pour out your hearts before him' (Psalm 62:8). That's easy enough when there is a strong sense of God in our lives, and our hearts are full of gratitude and praise, and good, positive feelings. But what of those times when 'negative' feelings predominate?

It is particularly important to share the emotions we consider negative with the Lord, such as disappointment (even anger) with God, bitterness at the unfairness of life, fear, desolation, grief, and confusing doubts. Sometimes we can make the mistake of thinking that we should only speak to the Lord of positive things and positive emotions, and so we bury the negative ones.

A sign of intimacy is when we can share our whole life, warts and all, with a true friend. The strength of the friendship shows itself in trust and openness. That's the sort of relationship that the Lord wants with us.

Therefore, strong emotions admitted, named and shared in prayer, far from blocking our relationship with Jesus, become part of that bond and deepen it. Speaking candidly about these feelings means our prayer is genuine. We are letting the Lord into our real lives and his love can flow.

Honesty in prayer leads to intimacy with God. Hiding our negative emotions and always having to put on a good face weakens friendships, including our friendship with Jesus. Then, our prayer can be just going through the motions; we grow distant from the Lord and our relationship with him becomes formal rather than personal.

The first person we meet in prayer is ourselves. Authentic prayer is showing ourselves to Jesus with candid honesty. Honesty is a sign of intimacy and honesty deepens intimacy.

The real person before the real God – that's real prayer!

Listening to his voice

On Mount Tabor, when Jesus was transfigured, the voice of God the Father was heard: 'This is my Son, whom I have chosen; listen to him' (Luke 9:35). A privileged way to listen to Jesus speaking to us is in the Scriptures, especially the Gospels.

There is a way of praying that is called 'sacred reading'. It involves reading a passage from the Bible in a prayerful, reflective way. We read slowly, not skimming over the words. We read lovingly as we would a letter from a dear friend. We read in order to hear the voice of the Beloved, to respond in love to his love.

We read gently until our attention is caught. A word, a phrase or an image may cause us to pause. When this happens, we reflect and ponder on what has struck us. One way is to repeat the word or phrase mantra-like, letting it sink in, aware of the feelings that are awakened.

We absorb the living word until it becomes prayer in us – praise, thanksgiving, adoration, repentance or petition – whatever way our spirit is moved to pray. We respond in simple prayer to what the Lord speaks to our hearts. We put words on our positive as well as negative reactions to what we read and we share these with the Lord. We let this prayer arise spontaneously so that the 'sacred reading' truly becomes a conversation.

The aim is not information but transformation. Better three lines pondered that speak to the heart than three pages read without true attention. Having many ideas about Jesus does not feed the soul. We are nourished when we taste interiorly the goodness of the Lord. An ounce of experience is worth more than a ton of theory!

We learn the heart of God in the word of God.

Uncluttered prayer

Cluttered times of prayer wear us out. Instead of being revived in body and soul, as the Lord wants, we can come away weary from our busy praying.

Some of us can feel we have to 'get through' certain devotions, novenas or whatever. There is nothing wrong with praying these prayers; however, if our prayer time is crammed full, we may need to reconsider what prayers we say. The Holy Spirit wants to lead us into deeper, quieter prayer. We need to be willing to let go of personal pieties when they no longer nurture us spiritually.

Again, many of us may need to look at our lists of prayer intentions. Petition is a fundamental form of prayer – praying for ourselves and those we love, and those we feel called to pray for. However, Jesus gives us some blunt guidance: 'When you pray, do not keep on babbling like pagans, for they think they will be heard because of their many words. Do not be like them, for your Father knows what you need before you ask him' (Matthew 6:7, 8).

We do not have to win God over or manipulate him with our many words. We are asked to pray in trust and simplicity before our loving Father. He knows our needs.

A simple way to unclutter is to say at the beginning of our prayer: 'Lord, all who are in my heart, I bring to your heart. You know their truest needs better than I or even they know them. I hand them over now to your limitless goodness.' We can intercede calmly for people by simply bringing them with us in faith and love into the Lord's compassionate and healing presence.

Uncluttered prayer refreshes the soul.

Patience with the Lord

All of us carry baggage, and all of us have faults and failings, inconsistencies and imperfections. When we begin to be committed to prayer, we expect change; and change does happen but not always as we expect it. Our patience can grow thin with God. 'I am faithful to prayer so where is the change in me? Why do I still have to put up with my short temper, my lustful thoughts, my self-centredness?'

The promise of the Lord still holds true. 'I will heal their waywardness and love them freely' (Hosea 14:5). He will indeed heal us, but in his own good time.

Jesus knows growth is gradual. When God wants to create a mushroom, he does it overnight. When he wants to make a great oak, God takes hundreds of years. The Lord views our lives from eternity. He is not in a hurry. So wheat and weeds can remain together in the field of our souls as grace works in hidden ways.

As long as the heart is turned towards the Lord and intent on loving, our failures are not the issue in God's eyes. In fact, the experience of his gracious compassion as we fall and get up again and again teaches us great reliance on his mercy.

Throughout it all, our hearts are being expanded to trust more calmly and to love more generously. As prayer deepens, we are able to live with a spirit of gentleness towards ourselves and others, even when our failings are, at times, painfully obvious. The gentle know that true growth requires nurture, not force.

The Lord is closer to us than we are to ourselves. Jesus knows us to the depths, and loves us as deeply as he knows us. In his tender goodness, he is patient with us and asks that we be patient with him, ourselves and others.

Seasons of the heart

Like any relationship, our friendship with the Lord, expressed in prayer, goes through different stages and seasons.

There are times when prayer comes without effort and flows with ease. We experience the Lord's closeness and receive helpful insights when we pray. These times of sweetness and light are not meant to be permanent.

At other times, we can experience a sense of dryness and boredom when we come to pray. Our enthusiasm for prayer wanes. The Lord can seem a thousand miles away behind a brick wall. We may feel forgotten by Jesus and wonder why we bother.

But these are the very times when our love is being matured and deepened. We are moving beyond just what we can get out of prayer to really wanting to be united with the Lord and his will for our lives.

Fidelity and perseverance in prayer at this stage are vital. It may seem to us that nothing is happening, but the Spirit is working in a hidden manner and with intense love within our souls – far below the level of thought and feelings. What we experience as absence and darkness is the presence of the Lord given to us in a new and more profound manner. In time, and with faithfulness, there comes a gradual re-awakening of the heart – a greater conviction of how unquenchable is the Lord's love, and a fuller awareness of all the ways he is present to us.

Our growth in prayer is measured not by experiences and warm feelings, but by fidelity and by an increasing gift of ourselves in love to the Lord and to others.

Whatever the season of the heart, we are asked to remain faithful to prayer.

Led by the Spirit

I have stilled and quieted my soul; like a weaned child with its mother, like a weaned child is my soul within me.

Psalm 131:2

Prayer is simple. At its heart, prayer is spending time with someone we know loves us. Like a baby secure and peaceful in its mother's arms, we are invited to find our repose in God. This depth of prayer has been called the 'prayer of presence' – a simple gaze of love between us is more than enough. Looking at Jesus looking at us – and smiling!

Prayer is simple – but we can make it complicated.

We can do this when we push ahead with our quota of prayers when grace is drawing us into silence, to gentle stillness in the divine presence.

Another hindrance to growth in simplicity in prayer is more subtle. This is the fear that can rise up when we become aware that the Lord is calling us to closer intimacy. We wonder: What will he ask of me? What will I have to let go of? Where will this end? It is important that these fears be named and brought to Jesus in honest prayer. We can tell him bluntly, 'I am afraid of where you will lead me!' This sincere prayer allows the Lord to calm our troubled spirit and give us the grace to take the next step with him.

It is normal that as we grow in our friendship with the Lord, our prayer deepens and becomes simpler. Then we realise it is enough to rest in his presence. We are content to be still and silent with Jesus. This attraction is a sign that the Holy Spirit is drawing us further into love. We can surrender in peace to this precious grace.

Be led by the Spirit!

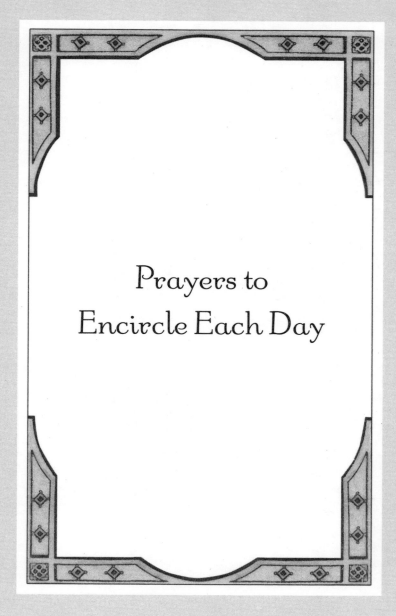

Prayers to
Encircle Each Day

Introduction
Be Strong in the Lord!

✤

Finally, be strong in the Lord and in his mighty power ... Grace to all who love our Lord Jesus Christ with an undying love.
(Ephesians 6:10, 24)

Daily prayer carries the Lord's strength into our ordinary living.

Our concluding section suggests prayers that can help us stay present and connected to Jesus throughout our day.

This section also includes some prayers that have been prayed with love and devotion down through the centuries.

Sunday

✦

As the day begins:

*Come with me by yourselves to a quiet
place and get some rest.*

Mark 6:31

*Jesus, on this day of rest may I open myself
to the refreshment of body and soul you
offer me.*

✦

Sunday

✤

At day's end:

*Do not be afraid. I am the First and the
Last. I am the Living One; I was dead, and
behold I am alive for ever and ever!*
                                   Revelations 1:17,18

*Jesus, grant me the eyes of faith to see
the signs of resurrection light and hope
around me.*

✤

Monday

✤

As the day begins:

I will never leave you nor forsake you.
Be strong and courageous.
Joshua 1:5, 6

Jesus, I believe you will be with me
throughout this day; may nothing take from
me the awareness of your presence.

✤

Monday

✦

At day's end:

The Lord upholds all those who fall and lifts up those who are bowed down.

Psalms 145:14

Jesus, I bring you any faults or sins that marred this day; let your merciful love raise me up.

✦

Tuesday

✦

As the day begins:

The Lord will watch over your life; he will watch over your coming and going both now and forevermore.

Psalms 121:7, 8

Jesus, I trust that my life and all it holds is under your loving gaze this day and always.

✦

Tuesday

✤

At day's end:

I will lie down and sleep in peace, for you alone, O Lord, make me dwell in safety.
                                        Psalms 4:8

Jesus, gift my weariness with restoring sleep this night; may I awaken with new openness to life and to love.

✤

Wednesday

As the day begins:

Take courage! It is I. Don't be afraid.
Matthew 14:27

Jesus, help me believe that nothing today is beyond your power and unwavering fidelity.

Wednesday

At day's end:

Trust in the Lord with all your heart and lean not on your own understanding; in all your ways acknowledge him, and he will make your paths straight.

Proverbs 3: 5, 6

Jesus, lead me in your ways, and still the anxiety that robs me of your peace.

Thursday

✤

As the day begins:

Let the morning bring me word of your
unfailing love, for I have put my trust in you.
Psalms 143:8

Jesus, I place in your care my heart, my soul,
And all the thoughts and feelings
that will govern my actions this day.

✤

166

Thursday

✤

At day's end:

I will bless you ... and you will be a blessing.
                                                    Genesis 12:2

Jesus, thank you for your abundant goodness to me;
Bless my whole being
And make of my life a blessing for many.

✤

Friday

As the day begins:

Show me your ways, O Lord, teach me your paths. Guide me in your truth and teach me, for you are God my Saviour.

Psalms 25: 4, 5

Jesus, I want to hear and heed your voice today; Help me build my life on the rock of your truth.

Friday

At day's end:

The Lord your God carried you, as a father
carries his son, all the way you went.
Deuteronomy 1:31

Jesus, your loving support has carried me
throughout this week;
I now put down any resentment, hurt or fear
that still burden me.

Saturday

✤

As the day begins:

You of little faith, why are you so afraid?
                                Matthew 8:26

Jesus, stretch my soul this day
with a new capacity to trust and to love
generously.

✤

Saturday

✤

At day's end:

You are precious and honoured in my sight,
and I love you.

Isaiah 43:4

Jesus, secure in your love for me,
may the seeds of gratitude and goodness
flourish in my heart.

✤

Name of Love and Power

Jesus, at your name every knee must bow.
Jesus, glorious name, gracious name, name of
love and of power!

Through you, sins are forgiven; through you,
enemies are vanquished; through you, the
sick are freed from their illness; through you,
those suffering in trials are made strong
and cheerful.

You bring honour to those who believe, you
teach those who preach, you give strength to
the toiler, you sustain the weary.
Amen.

St Bernardine of Siena

St Bernardine (1380–1444), the Apostle of the Holy Name, was an Italian Franciscan friar who spread devotion to the name of Jesus through his preaching. He popularised displaying the IHS monogram as a sign of faith and as an invocation of the Lord's blessing and protection.

A Short Litany of the Holy Name of Jesus

Jesus, Son of the living God, have mercy on us.
Jesus, splendour of the Father.
Jesus, brightness of eternal light.
Jesus, King of glory.
Jesus, sun of justice.
Jesus, Son of the Virgin Mary.
Jesus, Redeemer of the world.
Jesus, most powerful.
Jesus, most patient.
Jesus, most obedient.
Jesus, meek and humble of heart.
Jesus, lover of purity.
Jesus, lover of us.
Jesus, God of peace.
Jesus, author of life.
Jesus, example of virtues.
Jesus, zealous lover of souls.
Jesus, our God.
Jesus, our refuge.
Jesus, Father of the poor.
Jesus, treasure of the faithful.

Jesus, Good Shepherd.
Jesus, true light.
Jesus, eternal wisdom.
Jesus, infinite goodness.
Jesus, our way and our life.

Lamb of God, you take away the sins of the world — have mercy on us.
Lamb of God, you take away the sins of the world, grant us peace.
Amen

Ask and Receive

O Lord Jesus Christ, you have said, 'Ask, and you shall receive, seek, and you shall find, knock, and it shall be opened to you.'

Grant, we pray you, to us who ask it, the gift of your most divine love, that we may ever love you with our whole heart, in word and deed, and never cease praising you.

Fill us, O Lord, with a lasting reverence and love of your Holy Name, for you, who are Lord forever, never fail to guide and protect those whom you have solidly established in your love.
Amen.

The Origins of the Year of the Holy Name of Jesus

Devotion to the name of Jesus has been a strong element in Franciscan prayer and ministry stretching back to the time of St Francis, but was particularly fostered by St Bernardine of Siena in the fifteenth century.

2014 is the Year of the Holy Name of Jesus in Ireland for the Franciscans, the Poor Clare Federation and the wider Franciscan family. It commemorates the centenary of the renewal in Ireland of devotion to the Holy Name. The aim of the Year is simple – to foster a renewed reverence and devotion to the Holy Name of Jesus, and in so doing, to deepen personal love for the Lord Jesus and faithfulness to his Gospel. Pope Francis gave his personal support to this year.

In late December 1913, Fr Francis Donnelly OFM (1863-1929) gave the Poor Clare sisters in Galway a retreat. During the retreat he emphasised the power of the Holy Name of Jesus and also the devotion and zeal of St Bernardine – Apostle of the Holy Name. Fr Francis' preaching made a deep impression on the sisters; so much so that they erected a picture of the Holy Name in their chapel on the feast of the Holy Name in January 1914. This was considered by the sisters and Fr Francis to mark the beginning of a new wave of preaching and promotion of this devotion.

With the prayers of the Poor Clare nuns behind him and the example of St Bernardine to inspire him, Fr Francis embarked on a Holy Name apostolate. He promoted the practice of putting the monogram of the name of Jesus, IHS, over the doors of houses on blue tiles. Fr Francis set up a Total Abstinence Sodality under the patronage of the Holy Name of Jesus. He also organised the printing and distribution of Holy Name pictures, leaflets and badges, with the help of the Franciscan Missionaries of Mary.

This spiritual collaboration between the sisters, Fr Francis and other members of the Franciscan family in Ireland led to a surge in this popular devotion throughout the country.
www.holyname.ie

A Note on The Blue Tiles

As part of the wave of devotion to the Holy Name of Jesus, which sprang up in Ireland in 1914, many people identified their devotion by purchasing distinctive blue tiles bearing the monogram 'IHS' or 'YHS', which were placed above the entrance door to their homes. Examples of these devotional tiles can be found all over Galway, Limerick, Ennis, Cork and beyond.

'There's always been a kind of mystique surrounding the blue tiles, and also some peculiar theories as to what they meant,' says Galway Poor Clare, Sr Colette. 'This is a good chance to affirm that they do not indicate Garda stations!'

The custom of placing an IHS-monogrammed tile over the door of houses was popularised by the Franciscan friar St Bernardine of Siena in the fifteenth century. He introduced this custom as a means of encouraging people to practise Christian charity and to be peacemakers.

It was also a way of invoking God's protection upon the house-dwellers.

Our Mission in Zimbabwe

In 2008, the Franciscans celebrated 50 years of their mission in Zimbabwe. Irish Franciscans are present in South America and in South Africa, but Zimbabwe is the chief mission area for the order. The Franciscans came to Zimbabwe in the 1950s and following their ministry, some Zimbabweans joined the order: there are now 40 friars in the Franciscan Custody of Zimbabwe. The friars work mainly in rural areas of the country, helping to establish Christian communities, and have been responsible for building schools, hospitals and clinics there. For the mission of the church is not just concerned with the soul, but with the whole person. They are still inspired by the words of St Francis: 'God has sent us into the whole world, so that by word and deed, we may bear witness to him.'